WAS THE BUDDHA A SHAMAN?

a study of the shamanic faculties attributed to the Buddha
in the Pali Canon
and their implications for our understanding of Consciousness

By

Joy Manné, Ph.D.

1

Gombrich, in his article 'Eliade on Buddhism,' throws out of the window those elements in Buddhism that Eliade, in *Yoga, Immortality and Freedom,*.[1] Is Gombrich right? And what about other shamanic elements in Buddhism?

This short book starts with the problem of how to define shaman. As a solution it proposes a Typical Shaman's Case History. It then goes on to compare it with the historical Buddha's own case history as depicted in the Pali Canon to see whether there are sufficient features in common to justify calling the Buddha a shaman. It comes to the conclusion that there are. The implications are then considered with regard to two aspects of the Buddha's Teaching: 1. the problem whether the Buddha taught a metaphysics, and 2. the Buddha's Teaching on what is "not-self" – *anatta*. The paper ends with some observations about consciousness, including that it is naturally shamanic in its processes.

---

[1] Gombrich, 1974. His position is discussed in Section III, *The Death Rebirth Experience and Ascetic Practices including Heat*, below.

PART I
WHAT IS A SHAMAN?

The Encyclopaedia of Religion begins its article on shamanism, "in the strict sense shamanism is pre-eminently a religious phenomenon of Siberia ..."[2] Modern scholarship, however, is not limited to these particular shamans.[3] What makes Shamanism a problem is that it is currently a concept in evolution.[4] It no longer has a "strict sense," unless we arbitrarily attribute one.[5] Perhaps the best we can say is that the first scholars identified shamanism with practices in Siberia, but contemporary scholars and practitioners take a wider view.[6] Neo-shamanism is recognised and widely studied.

Scholars who are interested in shamanism come from fields as diverse as anthropology, religious studies, sociology, history, philology, psychiatry and psychology, and combinations of these fields.

This is how Nevill Drury, a contemporary anthropologist, defines shamanism:

> Shamanism is a visionary tradition, an ancient practice of utilising altered states of consciousness to contact the gods and spirits of the natural world. ... The shaman (is) ... a figure who through entering a condition of trance is able to undertake a vision-quest of the soul, journey to the sacred places and report back to

---

[2] ER/S:202.
[3] Gibson, 1997:39; Krippner & Welch, 1992
[4] Gibson, 1997:40f; Noel, 1997.

[5] See Krippner & Welch, 1992.
[6] See Gibson, 1997.

humankind on matters of cosmic intent. .. a healer, able to
conquer the spirits of disease .. priestlike. (Drury, 1989:1)

Roger Walsh, a professor of psychiatry and philosophy, tries to be
more precise and to provide a definition that excludes priests,
medicine men, mediums and psychopathologies – shamanism having
been considered a manifestation of mental illness in the ignorant past.
He defines shamanism as

... a family of traditions whose practitioners focus on voluntarily
entering altered states of consciousness in which they experience
themselves or their spirit(s), travelling to other realms at will, and
interacting with entities in order to serve their communities.
(Walsh, 1990:11)

Gibson proposed the following definition, which "will enable the
historical investigator to remain grounded in descriptive discipline:"

If a person is recognised by his own society as being in direct
contact with the divine or extrahuman (however that society
defines it) by virtue of concrete demonstrations of unusual or
unique capabilities, then he or she is a shaman. (Gibson, 1997:44)

For Eliade, shamans are also magicians, medicine men or doctors,
and may also be priests, mystics and poets, while all of these others are
not necessarily shaman.

The shaman is the great specialist in *spiritual questions*, it is he who
knows better than anyone else the numerous dramas, the risks
and the dangers of the soul. (Eliade, 1960:59)

5

The anthropologist Samuels looks at shamanism as a social phenomenon. For him it is:

the regulation and transformation of human life and human society through the use (or purported use) of alternative states of consciousness by means of which specialist practitioners are held to communicate with a mode of reality alternative to, and more fundamental than, the world of everyday experience. (Samuels, 1993:364)

Ellenberger, who was a psychiatrist, an ethnopsychiatrist and a historian, describes the shaman as follows:

Intermediary between the world of men and the world of spirits, the shaman exorcises, prophesies, watches over the life and the prosperity of the people, and cures certain illnesses, not to mention many secondary functions. (Ellenberger, 1993:330)

Ellenberger's special interest is the "creative illness" of the shaman. He compares the difficult phases Freud and Jung went through in developing their theories with this shamanic experience. I come back to this in my last chapter.

Although Drury, Walsh and Samuels use the general term "altered state of consciousness," Eliade describes the shamanic trance states as "ecstatic."[7] He distinguishes shamans from priests on account of their mastery of ecstasy[8] and defines shamans i.a. by their ability to enter

---

[7] See also Gibson, 1997:40.
[8] S:4.

ecstatic trances at will.[9] For Eliade, "Ecstatic" becomes a defining term for the shamanic trance states and shamanism is defined as a "technique of ecstasy," in particular, one in which "his soul is believed to leave his body and ascend to the sky or descend to the underworld."[10] Magical flight, being a psychopomp, mastery over fire and relating to spirits are features which Eliade attributes specifically to shamans. In their relationship with spirits, shamans do not usually become possessed: "the shaman controls his 'spirits,' in the sense that he, a human being is able to communicate with the dead, 'demons,' and 'nature spirits' without thereby becoming their instrument."[11] Further Eliade says the shamanic method of healing is unique:[12] the shaman searches for the soul and makes it return to the body;[13] he withdraws harmful magical objects and expels demons[14] and summons spirits to help him do this.[15] "The shaman is the great specialist in the human soul; he alone 'sees' it, for he knows its 'form' and its destiny."[16] Noel's discussion of the imaginal in these elements is useful.[17]

One of the reasons that shamanism is a concept in evolution is that contemporary attitudes towards it have changed and become more appreciative since Eliade expressed prejudice against it:

---

[9] Eliade 1958, 1964.

[10] S:4-5.

[11] S:6.

[12] S:5.

[13] S:182.

[14] S:215.

[15] S:301.

[16] S:8.

[17] Noel, 1997.

... If care is taken to distinguish shamanism from other "primitive" magics and techniques of ecstasy, the shamanic survivals that may be detected here and there in a "developed" religion in no way imply a negative judgement in respect to such survivals or to the whole of the religion into which they are incorporated. It is proper to stress this point, because modern ethnographic literature tends to treat shamanism as something of an aberrant phenomenon, whether confusing it with "possession" or in choosing to emphasise its degenerate aspects. .. (S:376)

Eliade was careful to separate shamanic phenomenon from their counterparts in Christianity and Islam, the latter being "better."[18] This early prejudice that "religion," meaning the major world religions: Christianity, Islam, Buddhism, Yoga; were "better" than shamanism has been reassessed in recent years.[19]

Another reason that shamanism is a concept in evolution is that today people are reclaiming their shamanic capacities.[20] As Eliade says, "No religion is completely 'new,' ... rather there is a recasting, a renewal, a revalorization, an integration of the elements ..."[21] Shamanic capacities are reclaimed in the context of our shared historical present. The recasting of shamanism is not due to "New Age" influences, however. The Encyclopaedia of Religions draws attention to

... [the] dramatic structure of the shamanic seance .. [its] elaborate staging ... [and] ... tricks ... reveal another world – the fabulous world of the gods and magicians, the world in which everything

---

[18] S:377.
[19] Gibson, 1997:40f. See also Samuels, 1993:8.
[20] Grof, Kalweit, Noel, Taylor, Walsh.
[21] S:12.

seems possible, where the dead return to life and the living die only to live again, where one can disappear and reappear instantaneously, where the laws of nature are abolished and a certain superhuman freedom from such structures is exemplified and made dazzlingly present. (ER/S:207)

It is not that Shamanism has gone "New Age," rather the so-called "New Age" has been influenced and, in part, created by the renewal of interest in shamanism![22] This is all the more obvious if we look at what exactly "shamanic ecstasy" is.

Shamanism and Ecstasy

Ecstasy is another concept in evolution through the work of Stanislav Grof, Charles Tart, Kylea Taylor, Ken Wilbur and others on altered states of consciousness including trance states. The question is whether there are altered states of consciousness that are particular to shamanism, as Michael Harner claims.[23]

As in the case of "shamanism" there is a tendency to make the concept of ecstasy very general and, as Walsh says very perceptively, "to equate shamans with masters of various spiritual traditions, especially Buddhism and yoga, and to assume that shamanic states of consciousness are identical to those of these traditions." Walsh goes on, "Such claims seem to be rather superficial, for the fact is that there is no one yogic or Buddhist state any more than there is one shamanic state.[24] He is, of course, quite right. With regard to this problem, Eliade proposes that, "The structural difference that distinguishes

---

[22] See Hanegraaff, 1996: 52f.

[23] Harner, 1980.

[24] Walsh, 1989: 227.

classic Yoga from shamanism (is that shamanism's) final goal is always ecstasy and the soul's ecstatic journey through the various cosmic regions, whereas Yoga pursues enstasis, final concentration of the spirit and 'escape' from the cosmos."[25] This is a very important observation as it attempts to delimit shamanism.

One important element that distinguishes the shaman's ecstasy is out-of-body experiences which the shaman can enter at will. These are signified by "the soul's flight to Heaven, its wanderings about the earth, or its descent to the subterranean world, among the dead." The shaman "knows the paths that lead to heaven and hell."

> He can .. act in the manner of a spirit: he flies through the air, he becomes invisible, he perceives things at great distances; he mounts to heaven or descends to hell, sees the souls of the dead and can capture them, and is impervious to fire. ... turn(s) into an animal, kill(s) at a distance, [and] foretell(s) the future. (ER/S:205)

During initiation and ecstatic trances the shaman dies symbolically, i.e. he leaves his body. This symbolic death demonstrates his ability to transcend "the profane human condition."[26] The shaman's ecstatic journeys make the world of the dead knowable, and "spiritualise" death itself which becomes evaluated primarily as "a rite of passage to a spiritual mode of being."[27]

The shaman makes ecstatic journeys for the following four reasons:

---

[25] S:417.
[26] Eliade, 1964 : 95.
[27] Eliade, 1964 : 510.

first, to meet the celestial god face to face and bring him an offering from the community: second, to seek the soul of a sick man, which has supposedly wandered away from his body or been carried off by demons; third, to guide the soul of a dead man to its new abode; or fourth, to add to his knowledge by frequenting higher non-human beings. (ER/S:205)

In order to enter ecstatic states the shaman uses various preparatory techniques including such ascetic practices such as fasting, sexual abstinence, exposure to excessive heat or cold, long periods of solitude, contemplation, meditation, and prayer, as well as dancing, drumming, drugs, the use of special costumes, and so forth.[28] Particular physical positions have also been shown to play a role in inducing trance states,[29] as has breathing.[30]

Eventually through practice and experience, the shaman "may no longer need prolonged preparation or external aids such as drugs and drums." Then "some of the qualities and abilities of the alternate state may become available in the usual state (so that) an altered state of consciousness becomes an altered *trait* of consciousness."[31]

There are many different kinds of shaman: the "shamans of yore" from many different cultures, and the modern shamans[32] through which the tradition is reviving and the definitions offered are more or

---

[28] Walsh, 1990 : 165.

[29] Goodman; Gore.

[30] Grof; Taylor; Manné, 1997.

[31] Walsh, 1990 : 164.

[32] Krippner & Welch (1992) and Noel (1997) provide an interesting accounts and critiques of modern shamanism.

less vague. We see better what a shaman is if we construct a Typical Shaman's Case History.

PART II
A SHAMAN'S TYPICAL CASE HISTORY

I introduced and explained the concept of the typical case history in previous research.[33] To resume briefly: case histories in psychology are records of how a person develops. When sufficient case histories are collected and compared, general remarks can be made about the aspect of development being studied, and stages can be identified. The general statement is a Typical Case History: it describes what we expect to be the course of development with regard to our subject. The subject can be the development of logic in the child which Piaget studied so fruitfully; the development of behavioural stages, such as Freud's oral, anal and genital stages; or the process of individuation, as studied by Jung.

The stages in the Typical Shaman's Case History are 1. *Birth*, 2. *Youth and Early Adulthood*, 3. *Initiation*, and 4. *Practice*.

1. Birth

Shamans may be selected at or before birth. This may happen through hereditary transmission, including deceased ancestors passing on their helping spirits.[34] If a shaman's child is selected at conception or birth to carry on the family tradition then particular rituals and preparations are required of the parents.[35] It is worth noting that gestation and birth

---

[33] Manné, 1995, i & ii. Then I used the term "hypothetical" but now I think "typical" is better.

[34] Eliade, 1964:28.

[35] Walsh, 1990:34.

are increasingly recognised as emotionally and spiritually significant events.[36]

2. Youth and Early Adulthood

Calling

If a person is not selected at birth or through hereditary transmission, the other possibilities for becoming a shaman include spontaneous vocation or calling. The future shaman may be called by spirits. Sometimes seeing spirits, which may be the souls of dead shamans,[37] is the determining sign of the shamanic vocation.[38] A person may also decide to become a shaman through his own free will. Self-made shamans, however, are considered less powerful.[39]

Spiritual Crises

There is a well-documented correlation between puberty and the shaman's calling, marked by a psycho-physiological breakdown at that time.[40] The youth and early adulthood of the shaman contain significant episodes or crises related to the calling:

The youth who is called to be a shaman attracts attention by his strange behaviour: e.g. he seeks solitude, becomes absent minded,

---

[36] See e.g. Grof & Zina, 1993; Manné, 1994, 1995; Taylor, 1994, Janus 1997, Chamberlain, 1998. Contact APPPAH for full information and list of relevant publications.

[37] Eliade, 1964:82.

[38] Eliade, 1964:84.

[39] ER/S:202-3.

[40] Gibson, 1997:46.

loves to roam in the woods or unfrequented places, has visions, and sings in his sleep. ... (He) has fits of fury and easily loses consciousness, hides in the forest, feeds on the bark of trees, throws himself into water and fire, cuts himself with knives. ... (He may go through an) hysterical crisis ... (ER/S:202)

Some of these activities are classical means of inducing altered states of consciousness or trance states.[41] The future shaman spontaneously evokes or falls into these. The potential shaman can also be catapulted into intense experiences after an accident or a highly unusual event such as being struck by lightening, or falling from a tree.[42]

A positive outcome to the calling and spiritual crisis happens when the crisis is overcome and the person is acknowledged as a shaman and reintegrated into society in that role. If the crisis is not overcome, the result may be insanity.[43]

3. Initiation

For those who survive the crises of calling, mentally as well as physically, the extraordinary events in youth are an initiation.[44] Elements in the initiation include ascetic practices.

Ascetic Practices and Death-Rebirth Experience

The traditional schema of an initiation ceremony is: suffering, death, resurrection.[45] The preparations for the initiation might include

---

[41] Walsh, Chapters 6, 12 and Epilogue.
[42] ER/S : 203.
[43] Gibson, 1997:46.
[44] ER/S:203.

"dietary modification or fasting, sleep deprivation, physical exertion and exposure to extremes of heat or cold,...meditation, yoga, ritual, prayer,...periods of quiet and solitude."[46] Drugs and hallucinogens are also used. These are all classical means of inducing altered states of consciousness or trance. The elements of the initiation may include: self-healing from the crises suffered in youth and early adulthood; dreams, including dream or ecstatic experiences of torture, especially the dismemberment of the body;[47] the ecstatic experience of an ascent to heaven or descent to the underworld; meetings with spirits; and religious and shamanic revelations. Mastery over fire and heat is significant.[48] An essential element in the initiation is that the shaman heals himself from his suffering. This may be from an illness such as epilepsy or from some other problem. Another regular event in the initiatory ritual is the symbolic ascent to heaven up a pole or tree.[49] Sometimes the initiation is a public event.[50]

The result of the initiation is that, "the new shaman displays a strong and healthy constitution, a powerful intelligence, and more energy than others of the male group."[51]

Teachers and Socialisation

Initiation includes an apprenticeship to a master shaman from whom are learned "both theory and practice: the myths and cosmology, rituals and techniques of the shamanic culture." In other

---

[45] Eliade, 1964:33.
[46] Walsh, 1990:30.
[47] ER/S:203; Walsh, 1990:59f.
[48] Eliade, 1964.
[49] ER/S:203.
[50] See ER/S:202; Eliade, 1964, Chapter 2, 4; Kalweit, Chapter 13.
[51] ER/S:203.

words, the apprentice shaman is socialised. His experiences are "cultivated, interpreted, and made meaningful within the tribal and shamanic traditions." Part of the training is journeying outside of the body:

> To become an effective Acosmic traveller he must learn the terrain of this multi-layered, interconnected universe in which he will quest for power and knowledge. He must (be) familiar with its spiritual inhabitants – their names, habitats, powers, likes and dislikes, how they can be called, and how they can be controlled. For it is these spirits whom he will battle or befriend, who will help or hinder him as he does his work. It is they who represent and embody the power at work in the cosmos, and it is his relationship with them that will determine his success. So the cosmology the would-be shaman learns is no dry mapping of inanimate worlds but a guide to a living, conscious, willful universe. (Walsh, 1990, p. 43)

The course of instruction is given both by spirits and by master shamans.[52] It comes after the shaman has received both the ecstatic training that enables him to dream and enter trance states, and the traditional training in shamanic techniques, names and functions of the spirits, mythology and genealogy of the clan, secret language, generating heat, etc.

Nature and animals

Animals play an important part in the initiation and after it. The shaman is supposed to meet with an animal during his initiation. That

---

[52] ER/S:202.

animal "reveals to him certain secrets of the craft or teaches him the *language of the animals*, or ... becomes his *familiar spirit.*"[53]

Recognition

Recognition that the initiation has been successfully accomplished comes when the shaman is acknowledged to have cured his illness himself.[54] It may come in youth, or it may be preceded by many years of training.

4. Practice: The shaman's work

After recognition, the shaman's tasks include teaching, journeying and healing, performing magic, relating to spirits, and a role in politics and society.

Teaching

Shamans tend to have experiences consistent with the myths of their culture.[55] They see the spirits of their culture, channel or act as mediums for their messages and train future shamans in accordance with the requirements of the culture. They teach and in particular contribute to knowledge of death. [56]

Journeying, healing and performing magic

The essence of shamanism, and what has been claimed to set shamans apart from other ecstatics, healers and mystics is the

---

[53] Eliade, 1960:60f.
[54] Eliade, 1960:76, 1964:Chapter 2; Walsh, 1990:Chapter 8.
[55] Walsh, 1990:116.
[56] ER/S:206. See also Krippner & Welch 1992), Noel (1997).

shamanic journey or soul flight in which the upper, middle and lower worlds are traversed at will.[57] Journeys are undertaken to learn, to heal or to help.[58] Shamans struggle against the powers of evil on behalf of their group.[59]

The shaman knows diagnostic and healing practices. He is a particular kind of healer:[60]

> Disease is attributed to the soul's having strayed away or been stolen, and treatment is in principle reduced to finding it, capturing it, and obliging it to resume its place in the patient's body. (ER/S:205)

Shamans perform magic, in particular flying, and travelling between the realms of heaven, earth and hell.[61] They remember their previous lives.[62] They have competitions.[63]

Relationship with spirits

Shamans have a variety of relationships with spirits.[64] The spirits may be the souls of dead shamans.[65] They may assist "with journeys, by providing strengths and abilities, by teaching, and by possessing the

---

[57] Eliade, 1964; Walsh, 1990:141.

[58] Walsh, 1990:142.

[59] S:509.

[60] See Krippner & Welch (1992) for an interesting discussion of shamanic healing.

[61] Eliade, 1964; Kalweit.

[62] Eliade, 1960:52.

[63] Kalweit, Chapter 15.

[64] See Walsh (1990:9, 130-137, and elsewhere) for a psychological understanding of spirits.

[65] Eliade, 1964:82.

shaman."[66] The relationship between the shaman and the spirits may be sexual.[67] While the shaman may be possessed by his or her spirits in mediumnic trance and channel their messages, most frequently he controls the spirits, "in the sense that he, a human being, is able to communicate with the dead, 'demons,' and nature spirits."[68] A shaman only controls a limited number of spirits. He may invoke the great gods to a seance, but that does not mean that he controls them.[69]

Politics and Role in Society

The shaman's political role is to defend the psychic integrity of the community, to be its anti-demonic champion, and to "defends life, health, fertility, and the world of 'light' against death, disease, sterility, disasters, and the world of 'darkness.'"[70]

Death

A shaman may die in a particular way:

(In) old age, ... many shamans again may undergo critical moments. Madness is said to be typical of aging shamans, and many of them die or "go" in their specific way "along the river of his clan without returning home any more" (Ohlmarks 1939). Modern society might call this having "committed suicide," but from the point of view of a shamanic society, it is a "voluntary departure," a normal end to a life which has been normally abnormal. (Pentikäinen, 1996: 7)

---

[66] Walsh, 1990:121.
[67] Eliade, 1964:72f; 79ff..
[68] Eliade, 1964:5f.
[69] Eliade, 1964:88.
[70] ER/S:205-206.

Summary

The Typical Shaman Case History is not particularly complex. He or she may be selected at birth. Otherwise, there is a significant incident or series of incidents in youth which may be psychotic or schizophrenic episodes, or what more aware contemporary therapists and healers call 'spiritual emergencies.'[71] The future shaman may be an epileptic or have some other major health or mental problem. The candidate is recognised to be a shaman through surviving psychically and physically several ordeals or through being able to cope with his ailment to the extent that he is considered to have healed it himself. In doing this, he acquires his basic skills and learns the basic knowledge that the group requires of its shaman, in particular journeying, healing and relating to the spirit worlds. After recognition the shaman's work in his community includes healing, teaching, performing particular magical acts, relating to the spirit worlds, and a role in the political life of the community.[72]

---

[71] Grof & Grof, 1989; Walsh, 1990; Chapter 8.

[72] The Shaman's Typical Case History is significantly different from the Hero's Typical Case History. See Campbell, 1949. (Campbell does not use this terminology.)

PART III
THE BUDDHA'S CASE HISTORY

To what extent can the Buddha be called a shaman? We can decide this through looking at the Buddha's Case History – the account of the events of the particular lifetime in which the bodhisattva became a Buddha[73] – and by comparing it with those of the Typical Shaman's Case History.

We do not imagine today that every detail in the story of how the Buddha became liberated or enlightened as presented in any canon is a factual account or a factual Case History. I am going to avoid the question of "early" or "original" Buddhism that is so well studied by Bareau, Bronkhorst, Frauwallner, Gombrich, Thomas, von Hinüber, Vetter, Zafiropolu and many other eminent scholars until the last section when I raise some questions and make some suggestions. Further, my study is limited to the Buddhism of the P-ali Canon and to the way these texts present the Buddha's life and work. My question in this section is whether this collection of texts presents the Buddha as what we would today call a shaman. If the texts attribute experiences to the Buddha that are obviously mythological, or that scholars generally agree are unlikely to be authentic, we must take it that the tradition wanted and needed these elements in its legend. Why that was, is an interesting question in itself, and I come back to it in Section VI.

---

[73] Despite Phra Khantipala's position that "a life of the Buddha…cannot well be restricted only to the last life but must take account of at least some of the previous lives in which the various qualities making for perfection have been developed and completed." (p. xxxi)

The Buddha's Case History as a Shaman's Case History

As in the Typical Shaman's Case History, I will divide the case history attributed to the Buddha in these texts into the stages of *1 Birth, 2 Youth and Early Adulthood, 3 Initiation,* and *4 Practice.*

1. Birth

The legends make the conception, gestation and birth of the Bodhisattva, the future Buddha, unusual and magical.[74] In shamanic terms, he was selected before conception. At least the texts consider that such an important person would have had a special conception, gestation and birth.[75] In particular, his birth is accompanied by extraordinary phenomena (glorious radiance throughout the worlds, the quaking of the ten-thousand-world system), and culminates in his being received into the hands of *devas* – i.e. spirits – before humans are allowed to touch him. Gods and wise men make prophecies about him.[76]

The legends also tell of traumatic events: the Buddha's mother dies seven days after giving birth to him.[77]

---

[74] MN Sutta 123. See also Eliade, 1960:110-116; Thomas, 1927, Chapter III; Seth, 1992:55-69. In Gombrich, (1974) certain elements of the Buddha's birth legend which Eliade has assimilated to the shamanic tradition are refuted. I do not use those elements in this paper.

[75] This is true for all Buddhas. DN, Sutta 14.

[76] Sn 131-136.

[77] The Buddha's Birth Trauma deserves study in the context of Birth Trauma Psychology (see Janus, 1997 for an overview of this subject) and I have this in preparation. Brazier (1997) is perceptive with regard to the traumatic effect on the Buddha of losing his mother so soon after his birth.

2. Youth and early adulthood

Calling

The Buddha's birth legend is that he was "selected" before conception. There are no accounts of any calling in the Pali Canon.

Spiritual Crises

The texts recount two episodes in the youth of the Bodhisattva which may be compared to the spiritual crises that a shaman goes through at the same period in his life. The first is an agreeable ecstatic state; the second is a traumatic initiatory crisis.

In childhood or early youth, at an age which cannot be divined through reading the texts which have different versions,[78] the future Buddha had his first intuition of a high altered state of consciousness:

> During the work of my father the Sakka, while sitting in the cool shade of the rose-apple tree, separated from desires, separated from bad things *(dhamma)*, I reached the First Dhyana, which is accompanied by thought and reflection, born from separation, consists of joy and bliss, and remained [there]. (MN I 246f, Tr. Bronkhorst, 1993:22f.)

This may be compared to a shaman's first, initiatory ecstatic experience.[79] It is noteworthy the texts have this taking place under a tree. Trees are significant in shamanic experiences.[80]

---

[78] Thomas, 1927, Chapter IV; Seth, 1992:79-82.
[79] Eliade, 1964:34.
[80] Eliade, 1964; etc.

The initiatory crisis or illness came years later. The Pali Canon tells us that before his enlightenment, the future Buddha asked himself,

> Supposing that, being myself subject to birth, having understood the danger in what is subject to birth, I seek the unborn supreme security from bondage, Nibbana. Suppose that, being myself subject to ageing, sickness, death, sorrow, and defilement, having understood the danger in what is subject to ageing, sickness, death, sorrow, and defilement, I seek the unageing, unailing, deathless, sorrowless, and undefiled supreme security from bondage, Nibbana. (MN I 163, tr. MLDB, p.256)[81]

Today we might call this an existential crisis – a crisis through confrontation with the condition of being human. Later – a different text tells us that it was at the age of twenty-nine[82] – while he was "still young, a black-haired young man endowed with the blessing of youth, in the prime of life," we are told that against his parents' wishes, he shaved his head and beard, put on the yellow robe and went forth.[83] The Bodhisattva's existential crisis occurred when or before he was twenty-nine, but we don't know any more than this about the age at

---

[81] Cf. AN I 145f.

[82] DN II 151.

[83] MN I 163, 240. Tr. adapted from MLDB. The expanded legend tells that the Bodhisattva had a luxurious life (see Gombrich, 1996:75f for a discussion of this legend) and was protected from birth from the sight of human suffering. When he saw for the first time an old man, an ill person, a corpse and an ascetic and learned that he too was liable to old age, illness, and death, he lost his enjoyment in life, and to determine to find a way out of a situation (being subject to old age, etc.) which he found unbearable.

which it happened. Thomas takes the word *dahara* (in MN I 163 and 240) to indicate that the Buddha was a boy when he went forth.

3. Initiation

The Bodhisattva's illness, as the texts describe it, was his inability to accept being subject to old age, illness and death. His attempt at self-healing, or the cure that he sought, was the way out of this suffering. In order to achieve that goal, he decided to leave home and become an ascetic.[84]

Nature and Animal Imagery, Good and Bad Spirits

The future Buddha's quest begins with episodes that recall the importance of animals and spirits in the shaman's initiation. As Bodhisattva, he leaves home on his horse. The horse is significant in Shamanism as a funerary animal and psychopomp and a means of achieving ecstasy.[85]

The account of the Buddha's attainment of Liberation, which defines the end of his period of initiation, is accompanied by nature and animal imagery. According to some legends it is attained under a tree[86] and in the presence of a serpent: the serpent king Mucalinda, a *naga*, protects the Buddha's head.[87] Serpents, *naga*s, and dragons are basic images in shamanic initiations and dreams. One of the

---

[84] Suttas that describe the going forth include MN 26, 36, 85, 100; AN, 3.

[85] Eliade, 1964:93 >From the most distant times almost all animals have been conceived either as psychopomps that accompany the soul into the beyond or as the dead person's new form.' See also p. 467.

[86] Vin I 1ff. See Thomas, 1927:68, fn.1; 70.

[87] SN I 124. V I 1ff. Thomas, 1927: 85. See Bareau, 1963:101-105; Gombrich, 1996:72-75 for a discussion of this legend.

recommended places for meditation is in a forest seated at the foot of a tree.[88]

Teachers and Socialisation

The Bodhisattva goes to teachers to learn how to achieve his goal.[89] Besides learning their methods and practices and their concept of Liberation, he also learns how to live as a member of a group of ascetics. He becomes acknowledged equal with each of his teachers and is invited to share the teaching with them. The Bodhisattva is becoming socialised with regard to the tasks of a religious leader. He is learning the rules. This can be compared to the apprentice shaman's period of studying with acknowledged shamans.

The Bodhisattva's teachers instruct him on how to attain particular altered states of consciousness, or ecstatic states, and he duly learns how to attain these at will. He learns to attain the state of nothingness from Alara Kalama, his first teacher, and the state of neither-consciousness-nor-non-consciousness from Uddaka Ramaputta, his second teacher.[90]

The Death-Rebirth Experience and Ascetic Practices including Heat

The bodhisattva is convinced that the altered states of consciousness his teachers have taught him are not the limit of what could be attained as they do not lead "to disenchantment, to dispassion, to cessation, to peace, to direct knowledge, to enlightenment, to

---

[88] DN I 71, and throughout the canon. See also Blackstone, 1998:94-102 for tree meditations in *Theri- and Theragatha*.

[89] MN s.26. See Seth, 1992, 104-106; Zafiropolu, 1993:22-29.

[90] MN I 163-166.

Nibbana"[91] and this is what he requires from the "cure" to his illness. He leaves his teachers and creates his own death-rebirth experience, going off on his own with five disciples for six years of austerities during which he puts himself through tortures almost to the point of death. In the words the texts put into the future Buddha's mouth to describe these painful experiences,

> I thought, "Let me, closing my teeth, pressing my palate with my tongue, restrain my thought with my mind, let me coerce and torment it. [I did this until] sweat came from my armpits."
> I thought, "Let me perform meditation without breath. .. I stopped breathing in and out .. there came about the extremely strong noise of winds which went out through my ears, .. shook up my head, ..[gave] strong headaches, ..cut my belly all around." (MN I 242-245. Translation taken from Bronkhorst, 1993:1-5.) [92]

The Bodhisattva thinks to undertake a total fast, but the gods intervene to warn him they will prevent it.[93] He compromises with a partial fast, taking food, little by little, drop by drop, until,

> My body became extremely thin,...my behind became just like the foot of a camel...my backbone bent up and down like a line of balls,...my ribs were breaking off and falling to pieces,...the glitter of my eyes was seen, deep and low-lying in the sockets,...he skin of my head became shrivelled and withered,...the skin of my belly

---

[91] MN I 166, tr. MLDB.

[92] Bronkhorst argues that the practices referred to in this and the following quotes are non-Buddhist and probably Jaina practices.

[93] MN I 245. See also Wagle, 1995:85.

had become stuck to my backbone.... (MN I 245f. Adapted and abbreviated from Bronkhorst, 1993:5-8.)

This is comparable to the shamanic dismemberment and rebirth experience, especially the shaman's contemplation of his own skeleton.[94]

There is a competitive element with regard to this fast:

The recluses or Brahmins of the past, the present and the future, who experienced, experience or will experience painful, sharp, severe sensations due to [self-inflicted] torture, experienced, experience or will experience this much at the most, no more than this. (MN I 246. Adapted from Bronkhorst, 1993:8f.)

This passage evokes shamanic competitions.[95]

Severe ascetic practices are typical in a shamanic case history. There are further details of the Buddha's ascetic practices in the *Mahasihanada Sutta* (MN, s.12) including,

I clothed myself in hemp, in hemp-mixed cloth, in shrouds, in refuse rags, in tree bark, in antelope hide, in strips of antelope hide, in kusa-grass fabric, in bark fabric, in wood-shavings fabric, in head-hair wool, in animal wool, in owls' wings. (MN I 78, tr. Ñāṇamoli and Bodhi, MLDB:173)

and

---

[94] Eliade, 1964:62ff.
[95] Kalweit, Chapter 15.

Dust and dirt, accumulating over the years, caked off my body and flaked off. (MN I 78, tr. Ñāṇamoli and Bodhi, MLDB:174)

The Buddha also avoided human contact completely, ate his own excrement, and inflicted extremes of hot and cold on his body.[96] Eventually, having gone to the extreme, the Bodhisattva rejects asceticism as not leading to his goal, or healing. Having survived his self-imposed tortures, he perceives that he is not reaching his goal through these severe methods. Remembering the agreeable ecstatic experience or altered state of conscience of his youth, he decides that that is the way to his goal. He succeeds, and becomes a Buddha. In shamanic terms, he heals himself.

Mastery over fire and heat is significant in shamanism. Images of heat recur in the Buddha's Teachings, e.g. fire symbolises the cycle of *samsara*,[97] and of course there is the famous Fire Sermon[98] and the event that precedes it I quote Gombrich who is remarkable for the breadth of his knowledge and also for the charm of his expositions,

In this episode the Buddha seems, if I may say so, to behave in a rather strange manner. There are texts (e.g. DN I 213) in which he says that he loathes the display of miracles. But here he performs a whole series of them.... The Buddha asks to spend the night in Uruvela Kassapa's fire house. The ascetic warns him that there is a *naga*, a supernatural cobra, living in there who may burn him up. The Buddha goes in and successfully vies with the *naga* in heating himself up, thought of course he does not hurt him. The

---

[96] Gombrich (1996:78f) remarks on the competitive elements in this sutta.
[97] See Blackstone (1998:102f) for fire imagery in the *Therii- and Theragaathaa*.
[98] SN IV 19 = Vin I 34f.

whole fire-house seems to be on fire (*aditta*) because of the heat the two of them generate. Moreover the Buddha's flames come in five colours. (Gombrich, 1996:70f)

Gombrich further explains that in the Rig Veda the name "Angi/irasa," by which the Buddha is called several times in the Canon, belongs "to a class of supermen, standing between men and gods, and Agni, the personification of fire, is the first and foremost "Angiras." He draws attention too to other texts where the Buddha is called "Angirasa" when he is said to shine very brilliantly. As Gombrich comments, "in this passage, (the Buddha) is virtually impersonating Agni, the brahmin's fire god."[99]

Eliade pointed out that MN I 244 speaks of the "heat" obtained by holding the breath, and that other Buddhist texts, e.g. *Dhammapada* 387, say that the Buddha is burning.[100] Gombrich rejects these two examples. He rejects the first passage on the grounds that it "is part of the Buddha's description of the *wrong* way in which he meditated before his Enlightenment; it is part of the mortification of the flesh which he rejects at the beginning of the First Sermon." Although the texts say that the Buddha rejected the mortification of the flesh *after* he attained Enlightenment, they give it *as part of his experiences on his path to Enlightenment*. Gombrich rejects the second passage on philological grounds and I have no dispute with his position here.[101]

As Eliade says, "'Mastery of fire' and 'inner heat' are always connected with reaching a particular ecstatic state or ... an unconditioned state, a state of perfect spiritual freedom. ... [It] indicates that the shaman has transcended the human condition and

---

[99] Gombrich, 1996:71f.
[100] Eliade, Yoga, p.331.
[101] Gombrich, 1974:226.

already participates in the condition of the 'spirits'"[102] The richness of the fire imagery connected with the Buddha and his Teaching is evident.[103]

Recognition

Recognition does not come instantly for the Buddha, except from the Brahmaa Sahampati. The first person the Buddha meets after his Enlightenment, Upaka, a naked ascetic, admires his complexion and appearance, but does not become a follower when the Buddha announces his Enlightenment.[104] Recognition comes once the Buddha has convinced his five companions in ascetic extremes that he has found what they were searching for, or, in shamanic terms, that he has cured his illness and can therefore also cure theirs.

4. Practice: The Buddha's work as shaman's work

We have seen in the Typical Shaman's Case History that the shaman's tasks include teaching, journeying and healing, performing magic and taking up a role in politics and society.

Teaching

Throughout the P□li Canon the Buddha is described in the following way:

An arahant, a fully awakened one, abounding in wisdom and goodness, happy, who knows all worlds, unsurpassed as a guide to

---

[102] Eliade, 1958, 332; cf.106; 1960:68.
[103] See also Gombrich, 1966:65-69.
[104] Vin I 8, MN I 170f.

32

mortals willing to be led, a teacher for gods and men, a Blessed One, a Buddha. He, by himself, thoroughly knows and sees, as it were, face to face this universe – including the worlds above of the gods, the Brahmas, and the Maras, and the world below with its recluses and Brahmans, its princes and peoples, – and having known it, he makes his knowledge known to others. The truth, lovely in its origin, lovely in its progress, lovely in its consummation, doth he proclaim, both in the spirit and in the letter, the higher life doth he make known, in all its fullness and in all its purity. (Tr. DB 1 78)

The attributes in this passage are also typically the attributes of a shaman: he knows the worlds, he has cosmic knowledge, and he teaches it.

The texts have the Buddha preaching sermons, taking consultations, and drilling his monks in his Teaching and method.[105] He initiates them into his practices. He asserts that he teaches a practical method that brings results:

Bhikkhus, this Dhamma is visible here and now, immediately effective, inviting (MN I 265 and variously. Tr. Ñāṇamoli and Bodhi, MLDB:358)

The Buddha's Teaching is founded on the method he discovered which succeeded in healing his initiatory illness.

Besides teaching his method, the texts have the Buddha teaching a vast diversity of subjects which shamans also teach. These included ethics, the world with its elements,[106] cosmology,[107] ontology (the

---

[105] Manné, 1990.
[106] MN, s.1.

beginning of things),[108] conception,[109] how things are born,[110] the nature of life (suffering, *dukkha,* and the escape from suffering) and a rather complete model of man (how consciousness functions, and what is not the self, *anatta).* The texts have the Buddha demonstrating knowledge of psychology: he encompasses with his own mind, the minds of other beings and people, and knows whether or not their minds are lustful, hate-filled, delusional, focused or disturbed, broad or narrow, with or without a superior, concentrated, or liberated.[111] Shamans are also psychologists.[112]

The Buddha sees with his Divine Eye He teaches through his higher knowledge, *abhiñña,* which has shamanic elements. *Abhiñña* includes such psychic powers as levitation, clairaudience, thought-reading, remembering previous incarnations, knowing other's previous incarnations,[113] and certainty of having attained Enlightenment.[114] Among the phrases used typically to describe the Buddha is, "He makes known this universe with its gods, *maras* and Brahmas, and the world with its wandering ascetics and brahmins, princes and peoples having seen it for himself through his own higher knowledge." The term *abhiñña* also occurs in an arahant formula. *Abhiñña* is an essential

---

[107] The Buddha's cosmology includes gods, Yakshas, Gandharvas (DN II 57), naming the eight great assemblies (DN II 109), and so forth.

[108] DN I 17f; DN s.27. See Gombrich 1996:80f.

[109] MN I 265f.

[110] MN I 265f.

[111] DN I 79f. See also Manné, 1995: 15.

[112] Kakar, 1982.

[113] S~riputta praises the Buddha=s way of teaching the Dhamma in regard to the last three in DN III Sutta 28.

[114] PED; see also Gethin, 1992:82.

development which occurs in many, if not all of those who succeed in following the Buddha's method.[115]

The texts attribute further shamanic behaviour to the Buddha. He teaches a spell.[116] He competes with spirits. He sees past lives.[117] He knows where people go after death.[118]

The Buddha prophecies. In the Panika Suttanta[119] the Buddha's attendant, Sunakkhatta, is full of admiration for a naked ascetic called Korakkhattiya who goes around behaving like a dog. The Buddha prophecies to Sunakkhatta that the ascetic would die of indigestion[120] *within* seven days and reappear among the Kalankañja, the lowest grade of asuras (minor deities, an unfortunate reincarnation). Sunakkhatta tells Korakkhattiya of the prophecy and asks him to eat carefully in order to prove the Buddha wrong. Of course, Korakkhattiya dies as the Buddha predicted. It is well known that when a shaman tells someone to die (or, for that matter, when a doctor does[121]), whether this is done directly, or indirectly as in this example, the person is likely to die. This even has a name in contemporary medicine where it is called the nocebo effect.

Journeying

One of the most repeated descriptions of the Buddha (the first quotation under *Teaching* above) says that "he knows all worlds." In the

---

[115] See Ergardt, 1977 and Johansson, 1969 for further discussion.

[116] DN s. 32. See Schmithausen (1997) for further discussion of spells, especially the Snake Charm, in Buddhism, and including "truth magic" (pp. 40, 49) and the protective function of friendliness (pp. 41, 49, etc.)

[117] DN II 91f.

[118] *gati,* MN I 73-77.

[119] DN s.24.

[120] Tr. Walshe.

[121] Siegel, 1986; Grof, 1993:192.

process of achieving Liberation, the Buddha remembers his former births, with clans etc., and those of others and knows their fate after death: whether they go to heaven or hell.[122] These are typically shamanic capacities related to journeying out of the body and soul retrieval.

The texts regularly have the Buddha travelling through the air. (DN s.25) He does this, and other shamanic acts, through his magical powers (iddhi):

> Having been one, he becomes many; having been many, he becomes one; he appears and vanishes; he goes unhindered through a wall, through an enclosure, through a mountain, as though through space; he dives in and out of the earth as though it were water; he walks on water without sinking as though it were earth; seated cross-legged he travels in space like a bird; with his hand he touches and strokes the moon and sun so powerful and mighty; he wields bodily mastery even as far as the Brahma-world. (MN I 69 & variously, Tr. MLDB:165)

These and other shamanic elements are an important part of one of the most frequent Typical Case Histories in the Nikayas, which I have called the *Samaññaphala Sutta* Typical Case History.[123]

Perhaps it can also be considered an element in the Buddha's journeying that he could make his voice heard through to the Brahma world or even further.[124]

---

[122] MN I 248; cf. DN s.4 for the Buddha's knowledge of other people's clans and lineages.

[123] Manné, 1995.i. When I wrote this paper I was not aware that elements in this Case History were shamanic.

[124] AN I 227. See also Wagle, 1995: 98.

Healing

The Buddhist Teaching and terminology is rich in metaphors of illness and healing. In various analogies a person who is not liberated is compared to someone who is ill,[125] and the enlightenment process is compared to a healing process. With regard to the Buddha's skill as a healer, in the medical imagery of famous arrow simile and elsewhere the Buddha is compared to a surgeon.[126] Elsewhere his Dhamma is compared to a clever surgeon.[127] With regard to physical illnesses, the texts have the Buddha teaching acceptance and detachment. He endured his own final ailment "mindfully and clearly aware, and without complaint."[128] The Buddha's healing is aimed at psychological and spiritual illness.

Performing Magic

The texts are ambivalent in their attitude to the shamanic powers related to performing magic and miracles. There are many more shamanic elements in the DN version of *Samaññaphala Sutta* Typical Case History than in the MN version, which indicates an important difference in emphasis between these two collections.[129] In the DN, the *Kevaddha Sutta*, (Sutta 9, §§ 4, 6) and the *Sampasadaniya Suttanta* (Sutta 28, §18) are contemptuous of many shamanic powers. The *Panika Suttanta* (DN s.24) is specifically against magical powers being the goal of the Buddha's teaching while at the same time being full of examples of the Buddha's shamanic powers, including demonstrations

---

[125] E.g. AN III 189.
[126] MN I 429; AN IV 340.
[127] AN III 238.
[128] DN II 128. Tr. DB.
[129] Manné, 1990.

of clairvoyance, a manifestation of his magical powers[130], and information gained from a spirit guide, namely Ajita, the general of the Licchavis who had recently died and been reborn in the company of the Thirty-three Gods. The display of magical powers in this sutta ends, as described by the Buddha, "I entered into the fire-element and rose into the air to the height of seven palm-trees, and projecting a beam from the height of another seven so that it blazed and shed fragrance, I then appeared in the Gabled Hall in the Great Forest."[131] The sutta ends with the Buddha explaining a full cosmology: the beginning of things.

The Vinaya has an account of a very long and intense magic competition between the Buddha and Kassapa of Uruvela.[132]

In the MN, in the *(khankheyya Sutta* (s. 6) monks are encouraged to wish or aim to attain the magical powers (*iddhis*), as well as the supernormal powers (*abhiññas*): clairaudience, knowledge of the minds of others, their previous lives, and the future incarnations of others. In the *Mahasihanada Sutta* (s. 12) the Buddha vaunts his magical powers (*iddhis*) and his clairaudience. It is through *iddhi* that the Buddha tames Angulimala the notorious murderer.[133]

Relationship with Spirits

Like a shaman, the Buddha has contact with the upper and lower spirit worlds, the worlds of the good and the bad spirits, of heaven and hell. After attaining Liberation, the texts have the Buddha expressing doubt whether to teach. Brahma Sahampati, who can be described in

---

[130] See Gethin, 1992:97-101

[131] Translation Walsh, LDB:380.

[132] Brekke, 1997.

[133] MN s.86. See Gombrich, 1996, Chapter V for an interesting explanation of this sutta.

shamanic terms as a good spirit, authenticates the Buddha's experience by coming to persuade him to teach.[134] The gods celebrate his first sermon.[135]

The Buddha is not only supported by the gods but also by spirits. When Saccaka, the Nigantha's son, does not answer a challenge, a *yakkha* bearing a thunderbolt comes to support him.[136]

On several occasions the "bad spirit," Mara, comes to try to persuade the Buddha not to teach.[137]

The Buddha is described as teacher of gods and men.[138] Gods, like humans, acknowledge his higher standing in their mode of salutation and in the terms of address they use when they come to see him.[139] They refer to his higher authority,[140] and ask him doctrinal questions.[141] They lend him their authority by confirming his statements.[142] The gods keep him informed: e.g. Brahma Sahampati informs the Buddha of Devadatta's defection.[143]

The Buddha controls his spirits; he is not possessed by them. He is a greater shaman than they are!

Competition

The Buddha competes with other shamans in various ways, as well as with everyone else who leads a religious group or holds a religious

---

[134] MN I 168f.

[135] Wagle, p. 88, SN I 421-423.

[136] MN I 231.

[137] Sn verses 425-449. See Thomas, 1927:71f and elsewhere.

[138] See first quotation under *Teaching* above.

[139] Wagle, p.86.

[140] Wagle, 1995: 91, DN I 215-223.

[141] Wagle, 1995: 84.

[142] MN I 497, Wagle, 1995:85.

[143] Wagle, p.88, SN I 153-4.

conviction.[144] In the *Kassapa-Sihanada Sutta*,[145] the Buddha claims to be the highest in morality *(sila)*, self-mortification *(tapas)*, scrupulous austerity *(jiguccha)*[146], wisdom *(pañña)*, and liberation *(vimutti)*.[147] In this sutta too, the Buddha asserts his proficiency in debates.[148] In the *Kevaddha Sutta*, he is acknowledged by the great Brahma to be more knowledgeable than he himself is.[149] This is another example of the Buddha controlling his spirits.

A particularly shamanic incident is the Buddha's competition with Alara Kalama. The Buddha is told that (one of his teachers) while conscious and awake did not see or hear five hundred carts passing close to him. The Buddha declares in his turn that he, while conscious and awake, did not see or hear anything when the rain-god streamed and splashed and the lightening flashed and the thunder crashed.[150] The text does not indicate what particular altered state of consciousness Alara Kalama and the Buddha were in. As Walsh observes of shamans, "During journeys awareness of the environment is significantly reduced."[151]

---

[144] Manné, 1990, 1992.

[145] DN I 174.

[146] The compound *tapo-jigucch*☐ is difficult to translate. PTSD has "detesting asceticism" under *jigucch*☐ and "disgust for" under *tapo*. Rhys Davids has both "austere scrupulousness" and "scrupulous care of others." Might this be referring to the disgusting ascetism e.g. of eating his own excrement referred to above?

[147] Tr. from Walshe, LDB:155.

[148] Manné, 1992.

[149] DN s.9.ɔ83.

[150] DN II 130-132. See Bronkhorst (forthcoming) regarding the authenticity of this incident.

[151] Walsh, 1990:220.

Some spirits defy the Buddha, but he proves he is stronger than they are.[152] He wins a knowledge and magical power contest with Baka the Brahma.[153]

Political and social role

The Buddha had a rich social and political role, despite the fact that he had gone forth and withdrawn from worldly affairs. He ran the Order of his monks. He was regularly consulted by kings, brahmans, leaders of ascetic groups and others. He was a confident debater in the eight assemblies, i.e. among nobles, brahmans, householders, recluses, the gods of the heaven of the Four Great Kings and of the heaven of the Thirty-Three, assemblies of Maras and Brahmas.[154]

Regular shamanic practice

After his Enlightenment, the Buddha continued the typically shamanic practice of taking retreats in the forest. At one point he defends this practice. It is not because he is *not* free from lust, hate and delusion but because it is pleasant for him, and to set an example. (MN I 23) He encourages his monks to practice in solitary places. (MN s.6)

---

[152] Wagle, 1995: 89.
[153] MN, s.49, *Brahmanimanta≡ika Sutta.* Cf. SN I 141-144.
[154] MN I 72, s.12. See Manné, 1992.

PART IV
COMPARISON BETWEEN
THE SHAMAN'S TYPICAL CASE HISTORY
AND THE BUDDHA'S CASE HISTORY

Previous studies have addressed the question of the authenticity of the information given in these (and other) texts about the Buddha with regard to his life, his parentage, the incidents supposed to have happened, and above all which aspects of the Teaching in these texts may be considered authentic – the search for Ananda's diary, as Frauwallner so wittily puts it.[155] To the best of my knowledge, however, there have been no studies of the *pattern* or *type* of life attributed to the Buddha, although Gombrich has described it as an allegory.[156] What, then, was this type or pattern? Was the Buddha indeed a shaman?

The following table compares the Typical Shaman Case History with the Buddha's Case History as in the Pali Canon.

Table of Comparisons

	Shaman's Typical Case History	Buddha's Case History
Birth	Sometimes important	Important
Youth and	Intense experience	Ecstasy

---

[155] Frauwallner, 1956:310.
[156] Gombrich, 1996:75f.

Early Adulthood	Crisis	Crisis: seeing old age, illness, death and the ascetic
Initiation	Apprenticeship Dietary modification Body dismemberment, torture Solitude Ecstasy, journeying - ascent to heaven - descent - meeting spirits Revelation Self-healing Mastery of fire and heat Animals and nature	Apprenticeship Dietary modification Fasting so severely that he was only skin and bones. Solitude - ascent to heaven - descent - meeting spirits Revelation Self-healing Mastery of fire and heat Animals and nature
Professional practice	Teaching	Teaching

	Journeying	Journeying
	Healing	Healing
	Magic	T + criticism of magic
	Ritual paraphernalia: drum, dress, bag, mask	Monk's robes, begging bowl, medicines, etc.
Death	Recurrence of crisis	? (Was it ongoing and needing regular "treatment" through meditation practice?)
	Suicide or "voluntary departure"	"Voluntary departure"

The Table of Comparisons shows the very close similarity between the Buddha's Case History and a Typical Shaman's Case History.

To what extent was the Buddha a shaman? Eliade's is still the best and most concrete (and so falsifiable) definition of shamanism that I have found. Eliade looks for a definition that does not confuse shamanism with "the mass of 'magical' ideologies and practices attested almost everywhere in the world and on all cultural levels."[157] He defines the following elements as being peculiar to shamanism:

---

[157] Eliade, 1969:319.

(1) an initiation comprising the candidate's symbolic dismemberment, death, and resurrection, which, among other things, implies his descent into hell and ascent to heaven.

The severe ascetic practices of the Buddha come close to dismemberment, birth and resurrection and correspond to this category.

(2) the shaman's ability to make ecstatic journeys in this role of healer and psychopompos he goes in search of the sick man's soul, stolen by demons, captures it, and restores it to the body; he conducts the dead man's soul to hell, etc..

Two elements in Buddhism correspond to this category: the Buddha's knowledge of what happens to people after death, and his statement that following his Teaching saves people from hell.[158]

(3)"mastery of fire" (the shaman touches red-hot iron, walks over burning coals, etc., without being hurt).

The fire imagery in the Teaching corresponds to this category.

(4) the shaman's ability to assume animal forms (he flies like the birds, etc.) And to make himself invisible. (Eliade, 1969: 320)

The Buddha assumes animal forms in the Jatakas. He regularly flies through space and makes himself invisible in the Nikayas and elsewhere.

---

[158] MN, s.130 and elsewhere.

The Buddha's relationship with spirits, here the gods and Mara, too, and especially his control of and superiority to them, conform to the shaman's capacities.[159]

The Pali texts attribute to the Buddha a shaman's life and life-style: they give the Buddha a typical shaman's case history. In every way, the Buddha as depicted in these texts conforms to Eliade's definition of a shaman. Further, as the *Mahapadana Suttanta* (DN, sutta 14) shows, they attribute the same life pattern or type to all previous Buddhas, so according to these texts, all Buddhas are also shamans.

What about the historical Buddha? Can we believe that he really was a shaman or did he go beyond shamanism? There is evidence for both in these texts. Some evidence suggests a certain ambivalence towards or opposition to shamanic practices, particularly those involving magical practices.[160] A large amount of evidence shows that the Buddha practised as a shaman even after his Enlightenment and his death was certainly shamanic. I come back to this question in the last section (7) of this paper.

---

[159] See also Gombrich, 1996:91.
[160] See also Brekke, 1997.

PART V
A SHAMAN'S EYE VIEW ON SOME OF THE
BUDDHA'S TEACHINGS

The extensive parallels between a Typical Shaman's Case History and the Buddha's Case History justify taking a shaman's eye view of the Buddha's Teaching. I will consider two problems here which this view illuminates. The first is the question whether or not the Buddha taught a system of metaphysics, and the second, the question of the Buddha's teaching of *anatta* – "not- self".

Did the Buddha teach a system of metaphysics?

The problem whether or not the Buddha taught a system of metaphysics has several aspects. One basic concern is how 'metaphysics' is defined.[161] Another element is how the nature of original Buddhism is conceived of. For the purposes of this paper, however, the interesting issue is that study of the texts leads scholars to ask this question. There is doubt!

A shaman teaches. That is part of his profession. His teaching takes the form of handing down the myths and culture of his society, both within the social group that he serves in a professional capacity, and, particularly, to aspiring shamans as part of their initiation. The texts which are presenting the Buddha as (i. a.) a shaman, have, therefore, to show that the shaman-Buddha has all the necessary

---

[161] Edgerton (1959) disputes Von Glasenapp's position. See also Thomas, 1929:192; Bronkhorst (forthcoming).

knowledge, and indeed they do so.[162] What is particularly interesting is how the texts depict the way the Buddha teaches metaphysics.

There are cases in which the texts have the Buddha teaching metaphysical elements reluctantly. The Patika Sutta contains a friendly and rather intimate dialogue between the Buddha and Bhagavagotta, a fellow ascetic (*paribbajaka*), allbeit of different practices. The Buddha visits Bhagavagotta in his park. Bhagavagotta makes him welcome and comments that it is a long time since he has called.[163] The Buddha describes some nuisance he has experienced with some particularly foolish and troublesome followers. He is exasperated with them and is grumbling rather freely about them to Bhagavagotta, as, one might say, between colleagues and equals who understand each other's problems because they are in the same profession. The Buddha recounts how Sunakkhatta, a dissatisfied monk, had complained that the Buddha did not teach him knowledge of the Beginning (*aggañña*) while, for his part, the Buddha had never maintained that that made up any part of his Teaching. The Buddha insists that of course he knows the beginning, and further, he knows things that go beyond that.[164] Moreover, he is consulted with regard to the Beginning by various sama≡as and brahmanas. The sutta has the Buddha refuting their positions and providing an explanation which they then embrace.[165] The Buddha teaches this reluctantly, but he teaches it nevertheless.

---

[162] See the section on Teaching under the Buddha's Case History.

[163] I understand from the text (DN III 1-2) that although he is a paribb☐jaka, Bhagavagotta has his own park (☐r☐ma), and that the Buddha is a regular, if infrequent, visitor.

[164] DN Sutta 24.

[165] See Gombrich, 1996: 80-82 for a discussion of how Buddhist cosmology is taught in comparison to and as a parody of brahmanical cosmology.

There are other cases in which the texts have the Buddha refusing to take up any position regarding metaphysical elements, as in the questions he refused to answer and did not answer. In still other cases they have him rejecting metaphysical questions on the grounds that they are "speculations .. which will have a particular result on the future condition of those who trust in them,"[166] "a net of views in which fish flounder."[167] The Buddha, rather, "knows things far beyond, ... He has , in his own heart, realised the way of escape from (these views), has understood, as they really are, the rising up and passing away of sensations, their sweet taste, their danger, and how they cannot be relied on, and not grasping after any (of those things men are eager for) he is quite set free." He has understood "those other things, profound, difficult to realise, hard to understand, tranquillising, sweet, not to be grasped by mere logic, subtle, comprehensible only by the wise ... which he has set forth."[168]

My position as a scholar is that the Buddha did not teach a system of metaphysics, but a practical method[169] which, as the texts so often say, led beyond the human condition, transcended old age, illness and death, and culminated in Enlightenment. It is completely logical that a method that leads to transcending the human condition has no need to explain or account for how things began, but only to explain how it is transcended. But shamans teach ontology and cosmology: it is one of their jobs. Confronted with such a unique and unusual shaman, what could the tellers of stories and the compilers of the texts do? The Buddha may or may not have taught a system of metaphysics. What the texts have him demonstrate is that he knows

---

[166] DN I 31.
[167] DN I 45.
[168] Tr. adapted from DB.
[169] See also Hamilton, 1998.

and understands other contemporary systems as well as and better than their own proponents – or should one call them his fellow shamans – do?

The teaching of "No-self" - *anatta*

A shaman enters into ecstasy or altered states of consciousness at will, and induces them in others for ritual or healing purposes and like a shaman, the Buddha did exactly that. He taught his followers how to enter altered states of consciousness (e.g., i.a., the *jhanas*) or trans-consciousness (*Nibbana*) in order to become healed of Suffering, craving, attachment and other aspects of the human condition that lead to unhappiness, and to become liberated from rebirth. His method can be clearly demonstrated through an examination of his Teaching on *anatta* - "No-self".[170] The style of this Teaching provides the method through which his followers could auto-induce a particular altered state of consciousness – the "No-self" state, at will.

I will not enter into the details of the controversy among scholars concerning the teaching of *anatta* – whether the Buddha actually taught that there was a permanent Self or that there was not one: there is already an enormous literature on this subject and I have nothing to contribute to it as it is argued. The "No-self" controversy is usually battled out between scholars on philological grounds.[171] I propose to take a "*shaman's eye*" view of this Teaching, in particular by

---

[170] This term is variously translated, including "Not the self," "Without self," "selfless," etc. My arguments in this section do not depend on a position with regard to translating or decoding the term *anatt□* as I take it to be a transpersonal experience and in this realm, describing altered states of consciousness almost always leads to problems with terminology.

[171] Bronkhorst, Collins, Gombrich, Oetke, Perez-Ramon, etc.

considering *how* the concept of "No-Self" was taught.[172] Before I turn to this, let me make some remarks about the Buddha's own self-concept.

The Buddha's own self-concept

At a recent conference whose theme was "The Psychology of Awakening: Buddhism, Science and Psychotherapy,"[173] many of the participants expressed their confusion regarding how the Buddha could function in the world *without a self*. Because they were Buddhists, they were trying to follow the Teaching and to achieve, or to imitate, what they imagined this form of functioning could be.[174] I thought they had missed the point! What the texts show in the character of the Buddha is someone with *a very advanced self-concept*. His self-esteem is perfect; he has gone beyond doubt; he knows, and he is confident of his knowledge; he expresses himself with conviction. When the Buddha talks of himself in the first person he does so with clarity. He has a strong sense of identity and knows very well who he is. He gives accounts of his life experiences in the first person. He gives accounts of his spiritual capacities in the first person: e.g. he announces and proclaims that he is a Buddha and says what a Buddha is. He gives first person accounts of the capacities required of him by society, e.g. he insists he is a competent debater.[175] He discusses at ease and in full equality with kings and other notables. He defends himself and his Teaching against unjust accusations and false representations. It is clear that the Buddha's 'self,' – as this concept is understood in contemporary psychology and psychotherapy: namely, a clear sense of

---

[172] See Bronkhorst, 1993:99, fn 12, and forthcoming.

[173] Dartington Hall, Devon, November, 1996.

[174] See also Epstein, 1988; Loy, 1992.

[175] Manné, 1992.

identity, the ability to function competently and realistically in the world, to have a standard of ethics, to achieve one's goals, to interact with people, to make good choices, and so forth – was fully functional and indeed remarkably well-developed.[176] Neither psychotherapy nor meditation is possible unless the sense of identity or ego is mature and well-grounded. Otherwise there is nothing to change and nothing to go beyond.[177]

What kind of a self, then, did the Buddha *not* have?

The context of the "No-self" Teaching

Ripinsky-Naxon maintains that "the idea of the surviving, or eternal, soul is fundamental to the tenets of shamanism."[178] At the same time he points out that the role that culture plays in shaping the nature of a preternatural experience has not been sufficiently studied.[179] The Buddha's Teaching on *anatta* – "No-self" took place in a particular context: the tradition of meditation and asceticism of the ancient Indian religious movements. This tradition can be understood as consisting of direct and consistent answers to the belief that action leads to misery and rebirth. In this tradition some attempted to abstain from action, literally, while others tried to obtain an insight that their real self, their soul, never partakes of any action anyhow. (Bronkhorst, 1993:128)

This background influenced the way the *anatta* – "No-self" Teaching was conveyed. Gombrich explains,

The Buddha's position...was opposing the Upanisadic theory of the soul. In the Upanisads the soul, *atman*, is opposed to both the

---

[176] See also Hillman, 1996, Chapter 2.
[177] Engler, 1984.
[178] 1993:37.
[179] 1993:19.

body and the mind; for example, it cannot exercise such mental functions as memory or volition. It is an essence, and by definition an essence does not change. Furthermore, the essence of the individual living being was claimed to be literally the same as the essence of the universe. This is not a complete account of the Upanisadic soul ...[180]

How the Buddha Taught *anatta* – "No-self"

Samuels compares "the death of the self involved in the Buddhist attainment" to "the ritual death and rebirth involved in many forms of shamanic training."[181]

The texts have the Buddha teaching against the existence of a permanent "self" through philosophical arguments which disposed of the positions of his adversaries.[182] They also have the Buddha teaching against the existence of the self through standard expressions, and through routine sequences of questions and answers. In this way the Buddha drills the monks to be sure they have understood his Teaching.[183]

Here are some frequent formulae through which *anatta* is taught:

1. This is a standard expression or pericope:

The eye is impermanent.

---

[180] Gombrich, 1996:16; see also the whole of Chapter II.

[181] Samuels, 1993:377.

[182] E.g. DN Sutta 1; Vin I 13f, and many other examples throughout the Canon. See also Manné, 1990:45..

[183] Manné, 1990:67.

What is impermanent is suffering; what is suffering is not the self; what is not the self is to be understood as it is with the highest insight (*pañña*) as,

'This is not mine, I am not this, this is not myself.'"[184]

The ear (*sota*) is impermanent ...,

The nose (*ghana*) ...

The tongue (*jivha*) ...

The body (*kaya*) ...

The mind (*manas*) ... (S IV 1 and variously)

The Teaching is that what is impermanent (*anicca*) and suffering (*dukkha*) is not the self. Here it is applied particularly to the six senses (*salayatana*).

2. This is a routine sequence of questions and answers.

"Is physical form (*rupa*) permanent or impermanent?"

"Impermanent."

"Is what is impermanent suffering or happiness?"

"Suffering."

"Is what is impermanent, suffering and subject to change fit to be regarded thus: 'This is mine, this I am, this is my self?'"

"No."

"Is feeling (*vedana*) permanent or impermanent..."

"Is apperception (*sañña*) ..."[185]

"Are formations (*samkhara*) ... "

"Is consciousness (*viññana*) permanent or impermanent?"

Etc.

---

[184] Translation after Gombrich, 1996:38.

[185] After Gombrich, 1996:4, fn.6.

"Therefore any kind of material form whatever, whether past, future, or present, internal or external, gross or subtle, inferior or superior, far or near, all material form should be seen as it actually is with proper wisdom thus: 'This is not mine, this I am not, this is not my self.'

Any kind of feeling, etc." (MN I 138f, tr. Walshe)[186]

Here the Teaching that what is impermanent and suffering is not the self is taught with regard to the aggregates *(khandhas):*[187]

3. This is a further standard expression or pericope taught with regard to the *khandhas* and the false view that they make up a self or personality – sakkayaditthi:

How does personality view come not to be?
A Well-taught disciple .. does not regard material form as self,
or self as possessed of material form,
or material form as in self,
or self as in material form.
He does not regard feeling ... apperceptions ... formations ...
consciousness as self, etc. (MN I 300, tr. Walshe, 398)

4. This s a further standard expression or pericope taught to avoid regarding the *khandhas* as the "self":

Whatever exists therein of material form, feelings, perception, formations and consciousness, he sees those states as impermanent, as suffering, as a disease, as a tumour, as a barb, as

[186] This sutta begins by rejecting philosophical positions about the self.
[187] See Gethin, 1986; Bronkhorst (forthcoming).

a calamity, as an affliction, as alien, as disintegrating, as void, as not self. (MN I 435 Tr. Walshe, 540)

5. Other ways at arriving at an understanding of what is not the self include cultivating the meditation on *Paticchasamuppada*.[188] It is through this sequence that the theory that there is a permanent self is grasped after. Through no longer identifying with this sequence[189] and overcoming it, this theory is no longer held.

Indoctrination, Induction and the Shamanic Transmission of Knowledge

Ken Wilbur argues that all valid knowledge consists of the following basic components:

> 1. *An instrumental or injunctive strand.* This is a set of instructions, simple or complex, internal or external. All have the form: 'If you want to know this, do this.'
> 2. *An illuminative or apprehensive strand.* This is an illuminative *seeing* by the particular eye of knowledge evoked by the injunctive strand. Besides being self-illuminative, it leads to the possibility of:
> 3. *A communal strand.* This is the actual sharing of the illuminative seeing with others who are using the same eye. If the shared-vision is agreed upon by others, this constitutes a communal or consensual proof of *true seeing*. (Wilbur, 1996:32)

In other words, the eye has to be trained to see; if it is not trained, it cannot expect to see (1). Once it is trained to see, it perceives (2). It then checks what it has perceived against the

---

[188] See Bronkhorst (forthcoming).
[189] MN I 66 and elsewhere.

consensus (3). Wilbur proposes that the way this works with regard to knowledge of the transcendental realm is:

> One first takes up the practice of *contemplatio*, which may be meditation, zazen, mantra, japa, interior prayer, and so on. When the eye of contemplation is fully trained, then *look*. Check this direct illumination with others and, more importantly, with he teacher or master. (Wilbur, 1996:34)

This could be a justification of indoctrination!
Gombrich describes how the Buddhist meditator has to train himself to see reality as the Buddha has taught it,

> In the fundamental texts on meditation, the *Satipatthana* and *Maha Satipatthaana Suttas*, the meditator has to train himself to see reality as the Buddha has taught it to be. He is to do this in four stages. First he learns to observe physical processes in his own and other people's bodies; then he learns to be similarly aware of feelings; then of states of mind. Finally he learns to be aware of *dhamma* ... the *dhamma* that the texts spell out are in fact the teachings of the Buddha, such as the four noble truths. The meditator moves from thinking *about* those teachings, to thinking with them: he learns (to use an anachronistic metaphor) to see the world through Buddhist spectacles. The Buddha's teachings come to be the same as (any) objects of thought, because anything else is (for Buddhists) unthinkable. (Gombrich, 1996:36)

Again it sounds as if the disciple is being indoctrinated! He is certainly being trained to perceive in the same way as his teacher.

What is particularly noteworthy in the passages containing the Buddha's Teaching of "no-self" quoted above is that they look suspiciously like *indoctrinations*! Although there are some cases of philosophical arguments against other positions,[190] there are many examples of the pericopes quoted above.

Why should there be so much indoctrination in an *ehipassika* teaching, where the disciples were invited to come and see for themselves, and by implication, to test for themselves? Bronkhorst has said,

> It is possible that early Buddhism did not deny the existence of the soul ... One reason why it did not want to talk about it may well be that conceptions of the soul were too closely connected with methods of liberation described in (non-Buddhist meditation). (Bronkhorst, 1993:99, fn.12.)

It is well-known that hypnosis is easily induced when there is sensory deprivation or sensory repetition.[191] Meditation requires sensory deprivation. Moreover there is sensory repetition, for example, in observing the breathing, which is basic to Buddhist meditation practice.[192] My proposition is that these passages are not so much indoctrinations – although they do, in fact, in-doctrinate – as much as **inductions**. They serve as self-suggestion, or auto-hypnotic messages[193] designed to induce a particular altered state of consciousness, namely, that of "no-self." When the monks sat down

---

[190] Gombrich, 1996, Chapter II.

[191] Cheek, 1994:28.

[192] Manné, 1994, 1995, 1997.

[193] See Staal, 1975. Staal discusses earlier work by S. Lindquist.

to meditate (perhaps at the foot of a tree), having learned by heart, studied and been in-doctrinated into the ideas expressed in the passages above and in other similar passages, they would tell themselves with regard to all of their experiences as they arose "This is not the 'self'" or "This is not mine, I am not this, this is not myself." They would be using one of the many available *anatta* – "No-self" experience inductions. Eventually all that would be left to those among them for whom these inductions worked would be the experience of the altered state of consciousness of "No-self."

One of the shaman's tasks is to induce his followers into altered states of consciousness.[194] This is one of the ways in which he transmits his knowledge. Many elements in the Buddha's method are capable of inducing shamanic states of consciousness. These include solitude, moderate eating (Vinaya shows how few monks could cope with the periods of fasting), sensory deprivation, and Breathwork (Anapa*nasati Sutta*). Felicitas Goodman, in her extraordinary work on trance and posture, has already shown that when trance is induced, "without an absolute commitment to a mythology, ... there (is) nothing to give cohesion to the experiences....The trance experience itself is vacuous....If no belief system is proffered, it will remain vacuous."[195] The shamanic trance experience requires a belief system to give it its meaning.

The formulations of the "no-self" Teaching were the Buddha's way of leading his followers into an experience that was consistent with his Teaching. The followers had to be in-doctrinated first, and

---

[194] Drury, 1982:18. On the use of the breath as an induction, see Grof, 1988.

[195] Goodman, 1990, p.17. Goodman quotes the work of V. F. Emerson who "had done work with various meditative disciplines and had found that differences in their belief systems correlated with the fact that during meditation, each discipline employed its own specific body posture."

clear inductions into the required state had to be given, because, as Bronkhorst, Gombrich and others have said, the Buddha's position and that of the brahmins was very close – close enough for Gombrich to call whether or not the Buddha believed in a self a pseudo-problem.[196] The Buddha had to in-doctrinate his monks to make sure they had the "right" experience.

The texts have the Buddha saying,

> Potthapada, it is difficult for one of different views, a different faith, under different influences, with different pursuits and a different training to know whether these [perception and the self] are two different things or not. (DN I, s.9; LDB 164; cf. DN s.24, 25)

The inductions alone were not enough. Simply practising the inductions did not necessarily lead to the ecstatic, or trance, or altered state of consciousness experience of "no-self" which the Buddha, as shaman, offered to his followers as a cure for their suffering. In-doctrination was essential as the Buddha's "no-self" inductions could as easily lead the practitioner to the experience of the Self in the Brahmanical or Jungian sense as to the "no-self" experience that the Buddha taught. They could just as easily lead a disciple to enter the ecstatic state offered by a rival shaman.

---

[196] Gombrich, 1996:64.

PART VI
SHAMANISM, BUDDHISM AND CONSCIOUSNESS

The Pali Canon presents the Buddha as a shaman. Etymologically, the word "shaman" is derived from the word s[h]*ramana/ samana*[197] and several different Buddhist words have come to used to refer to the shaman in different cultures. Gibson argues that this is not due to "a single wave of wave of cultural influence, but must be seen as a process that was repeated several times." Gibson further argues that the linguistic evidence demonstrates Buddhism's intimate concern with the special qualities that distinguish the shaman.[198] This is supported by the strong similarities between the Buddha's Case History and the Typical Shaman's Case History.

Propaganda and the Communication of the Teaching

Did the texts have to present the Buddha as a shaman for propaganda purposes in order to make their hero and their message more convincing? The possession of at least some shamanic capacities certainly seems essential and indeed inevitable in a religious leader. As Samuels has pointed out, "Major world religions such as Buddhism,

---

[197] Gibson, 1997:51. Paul Kiparsky, personal communication (email, 7th March, 1997): 'According to Vasmer's Russisches Etymologisches Woerterbuch, Russian *shaman* is ultimately from Prakrit *samana*. He thinks it was borrowed into Russian via Tungic *shaman* "Buddhist Monk" and Tocharian *shamane*. The Western European languages might have got the word either from Russian or via Persian." But see also Ripinsky-Naxon, 1993:69.
[198] Gibson, 1997:50f.

Islam, and Christianity frequently derive their initial impetus from a 'shamanic'-style revelation."[199]

The oral tradition and, eventually the texts themselves, had to make the Teaching communicable. So, of course, did the Buddha, when he started teaching. As Zafiropulo has said about the basic requirements for communicating the Teaching,

> Une prédication[s], qui, dès son début se sera déplacée dans une aire aussi vaste et un milieu linguistique de ce genre, aura forcément dû pour se faire comprendre
>   1) s'adapter continuellement, à mesure qu'elle se déplaçait, aux situations dialectales locales;
>   2) utiliser un vocabulaire déjà existant, avec termes et concepts accessibles à tous;
>   et, si le besoin de forger quelque « mot-concept » nouveau se faisait sentir, de le faire d'une manière intelligible pour tous... (p.19)

Samuels sees early Buddhism "as an attempt to create a framework that could reconcile the literate, rationalised, hierarchical society that was coming into being with the human values of the older, shamanic form of society" and the Buddha's Teachings as "an adaptation of the shamanic training for the new urban social context."[200] The Buddha's case history as conveyed by the Pali texts demonstrates a substantial shamanic element in the religious milieu of the Buddha's time and for several later centuries. Otherwise attributing to the Buddha a shamanic development – a shaman's birth, youth and young adulthood, initiation and life – would have made no sense and

---

[199] Samuels, 193:365.
[200] Samuels, 1993:365, 368ff.

would have convinced and converted no-one. If the Buddha, or the tradition (as we have inherited it in the Pali texts) wanted to convince these groups that he, or it, had a better method, it was essential to have shamanic elements in the texts. It was also essential to present the Buddha as a more powerful "shaman" than any of the others around, and, indeed, this is what the texts do.

To say, however, that the shamanic elements are in the texts for propaganda purposes, does not explain them away.

Consciousness is naturally shamanic

Pentikäinen says, "The concept of shamanism has undergone a kind of devaluation in recent popular and scientific literature....Shamanism is nowadays offered as a universal means of penetrating into the depths of the human conscience."[201] Pentikäinen is wrong. The concept "shamanism" has not undergone a *devaluation* but a *re-evaluation,* and a very healthy, positive and inspiring re-evaluation at that.[202]

Shamanism has come back into our contemporary societies in many different ways during the last twenty or thirty years, from attempts to learn from contemporary shamans, to attempts to discover and recreate original shamanic practices (as if that were really possible), to the recognition of placebo effects and nocebo effects, to teaching doctors how to use beneficially the healing powers their patients attribute to them,[203] to the revival of magical practices, the

---

[201] Pentikäinen, 1996: 6.

[202] See e.g. Krippner & Welch (1992), Noel (1997).

[203] Personal communication from a pediatrician in Lausanne, Switzerland regarding post-qualification courses on offer.

recognition of the effect of hands-on healing and prayer[204] – the list is endless.

Andrew Weil proposes that, "We seem to be born with a drive to experience episodes of altered consciousness," and that, "this drive expresses itself at very early ages in all children in activities designed to cause loss or major disturbances of ordinary awareness."[205]

Walsh has pointed out that most cultures have "institutionalized altered states of consciousness." He argues that conditions that induce shamanic states ".. include such common experiences as isolation, fatigue, hunger, and rhythmic sound, and thus they are likely to be discovered by different generations and cultures." He too proposes that "shamanism and its widespread distribution may reflect an innate human tendency to enter certain pleasurable and valuable states of consciousness," and that "Once discovered, rituals and beliefs that support the induction and expression of these states would also arise and shamanism would emerge once again."[206]

Walsh and Weil are idealizing. If it is a natural human tendency to enter into shamanic states, it is as natural to enter into the terrifying states as into the agreeable ones – and it may even be more natural![207] Ellenberger's concept of the creative illness supports this position.

In *The Discovery of the Unconscious*, Ellenberger compares the shaman's "initiatory illness" to "creative illnesses," as he designates "the experiences of certain mystics, poets and philosophers."[208] Ellenberger defines a "creative illness" as follows,

---

[204] Dossey, 1997.

[205] Weil, 1972 : 23.

[206] Walsh, 1990 : 14.

[207] Grof, 1988.

[208] Ellenberger, 1970 : 39.

A creative illness succeeds a period of intense preoccupation with an idea and search for a certain truth. It is a polymorphous condition that can take the shape of depression, neurosis, psychosomatic ailments, or even psychosis. Whatever the symptoms, they are felt as painful, if not agonizing, by the subject, with alternating periods of alleviation and worsening. Throughout the illness the subject never loses the thread of his dominating preoccupation. It is often compatible with normal, professional activity and family life. But even if he keeps to his social activities, he is almost entirely absorbed with himself. He suffers from feelings of utter isolation, even when he has a mentor who guides him through the ordeal (like the shaman apprentice with his master.) The termination is often rapid and marked by a phase of exhilaration. The subject emerges from his ordeal with a permanent transformation in his personality and the conviction that he has discovered a great truth or a new spiritual world. (Ellenberger, 1970 : 890)

Ellenberger is discussing elements in the development of the great psychiatrists, Freud and Jung and comparing them to the general pattern of shamanic development.[209] He distinguishes between the creative illnesses of the pathfinders and the followers,

The pathfinder should not only teach the theory but provide a practical guide for others to follow that theory. Thus the shaman-apprentice must see an old shaman, at regular intervals, whose instruction he will put into practice step by step throughout his initiatory malady. (Ellenberger, 1970 : 890)

---

[209] Ellenberger, 1970 : 889.

The specific character of the creative illness is that,

> It is a strictly personal experience for its pathfinder, but it sets a
> model for the follower, and this conformity of pattern will tend
> to be transmitted from one initiated to the other within the same
> school. (Ellenberger, 1970 : 891)

It is well-known that the clients of analysts are followers and
show conformity of pattern: they produce dreams in accordance with
their analyst's school!

Walsh takes the position that "some recurring combination of
social forces and innate abilities must have repeatedly elicited and
maintained shamanic roles, rituals, and states of consciousness."[210] For
Jung "shamanic symbolism is a projection of the individuation
process."[211] Janus describes the shaman's journey as "a graphic
reactivation and symbolization of pre- and perinatal experience"[212]
Weil maintains that we are born with a drive to experience altered
states of consciousness.[213] Noel shows the relationship between
shamanism and the imagination, discussing contemporary
shamanovelists and shamanthropologists.[214] My argument is that
consciousness is naturally shamanic. As naturally and as inevitable
as consciousness tends to create the experience of Ego or
individuality, consciousness equally naturally tends to create and to
seek shamanic experiences. It has, quite naturally and of itself, a

---

[210] Walsh, 1989:7-8; 1990 : 14.

[211] Jung, 1954:341. See also Downton, 1989:73.

[212] Janus, 1997:165

[213] Janus, 1997. See also Ripinsky-Naxon, 1993:94, 133.

[214] Noel, 1997.

shamanic dimension.[215] Further, as shamanism is culturally influenced in its manifestation, this also accounts for the large variety of its different manifestations, and also for why it is difficult to define it with complete precision. Moreover, it is healthy and healing for consciousness to be shamanic, as Frances Vaughan says, "The popular resurgence of interest in shamanism has given many people an opportunity to see themselves in a new light, validating the spiritual dimension of experience and reconnecting them to nature in a meaningful way."[216] It may indeed be that for creativity, invention and healing to take place, it is essential for consciousness to have access to its shamanic dimension. Even those with the most hard-core materialist view of consciousness, Dennett and his colleagues, have taken the bat as their shamanic animal – although they have not – as yet – succeeded in communicating with it![217]

What about the much discussed relationship between shamanism and mental disease?[218] This is what Walsh says,

What can we make of this curious combination of initial disturbance and subsequent health? Mainstream psychiatry rarely recognizes the possibility of positive outcomes from psychosis;

---

[215] See also Dourley on Jung and shamanism, p. 54. It is possible that Burkert is saying the same thing, although in different language, when he says, "Religion (is) an aboriginal tradition of serious communication with powers that cannot be seen. The problem of 'worlds beyond' .. (can be accounted for through) the existence of biological patterns of actions, reactions, and feelings activated and elaborated through ritual practice and verbalized teachings, with anxiety playing a foremost role. Religion offers solutions to various critical situations recurring in individual lives." (1996 : 177)

[216] Vaughan, 1995 : 116. See also Kalweit, Chapter 19.

[217] Dennett, 1991 : 441-448; Akins, 1993 : 151f.

[218] Eliade, 1964; Grof & Grof, 1989; Kalweit, Part 5; Walsh, 1990, Chapter 8; etc.

the diagnostic manual does not even mention it.[219] ... Yet a significant number of researchers, some quite eminent, have recognized that psychological disturbances, even including psychoses, may function as growth experiences that result in greater psychological or spiritual well-being. (Walsh, 1990 : 90)[220]

These crises are currently called transpersonal crises, spiritual emergency or spiritual emergence.[221] Shamanic societies, and now many New Age groups provide a framework for these experiences. Walsh says

Mystical traditions serve as road maps for using (the) technology (of the sacred) ... From this perspective we might say that mystical traditions and religions are created and sustained by people who access transcendent states of consciousness and then provide instructions whereby others can also access them and thereby re-create the founder's insights. ... Ideally, mystical traditions serve to preserve and transmit these insights and instructions.

Where Walsh says that "The first such tradition was shamanism,"[222] I wish to add, "and the last."[223]

Consciousness is naturally shamanic. The whole "New Age" movement in its wonderful and in its terrible forms, including the contemporary drug culture illustrates this.

---

[219] Since then DSM IV has introduced the category, that of Religious and Spiritual Problems, which at least opens the door to this possibility.

[220] See also Eliade, 1960 : 76-80.

[221] Walsh, 1990 : 93; Grof & Grof, 1989; Grof & Bennett, 1993; Perry 1974.

[222] Walsh, 1990 : 160.

[223] See Noel (1997) for an appraisal and a critique of how neoshamanism is developing.

Considered from its own point of view, all the strange behaviour of the shaman reveals the highest spirituality; it is, in fact, expressive of an ideology which is coherent and of great nobility. The myths by which this ideology is constituted are among the most beautiful and profound in existence: they are the myths of Paradise and the Fall, of the immortality of primordial man and his conversation with God, or the origin of death and the discovery of the *spirit* in every sense of the word. (Eliade, 1960 : 70)

The New Age movement has nothing new about it. It is simply consciousness reasserting its essential nature, and its quest to return to paradise.

PART VII
GOING BEYOND SHAMANISM

I come back to the discussion (at the end of section 4) whether the Buddha was indeed a shaman or whether he did, in fact, go beyond shamanism? The texts attest beyond any doubt that the Buddha practised as a shaman. How, therefore, do we account for those instances when the texts depict the Buddha as turning against certain shamanism elements and practices? Was he simply removing shamanic elements that were not necessary to his own self-healing, and therefore to his (shamanic) method? As Bronkhorst says, the Buddha claimed to teach something new.[224] Was an element in this new method the fact that it led beyond shamanism? If it was, becoming shamanic was a stage through which the Buddha passed before he went beyond it. Lee Siegel, however, says,

> The sannyasi is precisely he who sees through illusions, through all tricks, all magic; he is the man for whom nothing is surprising, who feels no wonder. Thus his liberation from this world. (1991:412)

If he is right, then going beyond the shaman's tricks and magic is not the new element in the Buddha's Teaching, but is something common to all sannyasis, or at least to those that achieve liberation.

Was the Buddha a shaman? Yes, the evidence is clear: the Buddha practised in a way comparable to the practices of a shaman. Did the Buddha go beyond shamanism? I don't think the evidence is clear enough. There are some passages in which the Buddha is depicted as

---

[224] Bronkhorst, 1993.

being against shamanic practices, but these are rather few, while the Buddha is depicted as performing shamanic practices throughout his life time.

What I propose is that consciousness is naturally shamanic in its processes. It is natural for people who are following a spiritual path to conceive of it, or to construct it in the shamanic terms of initiations and tests and developing higher powers. It is equally natural for them to develop some shamanic capacities, those that perhaps they are explicitly seeking, and others that come, of themselves; and it does not seem to matter which spiritual path they follow. Some people stop there.

The Buddhist texts indicate that the Buddha did not stop there, but went – as Lee Siegel suggests other sannyasis have gone before him – beyond it.[225]

---

[225] See Bronkhorst 2012 on Absorption for an important explanation.

BIBLIOGRAPHY

Akins, Kathleen (1993), 'What is it Like to be Boring and Myopic?' in Dahlbom, Bo (ed.) (1993), *Dennett and his Critics*. Oxford: Blackwell, 1995.

APPAH - Association for Pre- and Perinatal Psychology and Health, Central Office, 340 Colony Road, Box 994, Geyserville, CA 95441, USA

Batchelor, Stephen (1994), The Awakening of the West: the encounter of Buddhism and Western Culture. Berkeley, California: Parallax Press.

Blackstone, Kathryn R. (1998), Women in the Footsteps of the Buddha: Struggle for Liberation in the Theiiāgaatha. Richmond, Surrey: Curzon, 1998.

Brazier, David (1997), The Healing Buddha: a Buddhist Psychology of Character, Adversity and Passion. London : Constable.

Brekke, Torkel, 'The Early Sangha and the Laity.' *Journal of the International Association of Buddhist Studies*, Volume 20, Number 2.

Bronkhorst, Johannes (1993), *The Two Traditions of Meditation in Ancient India*. Delhi: Motilal Banarsidass (2nd edition)

Bronkhorst, Johannes (forthcoming), 'Die Buddhistische Lehre.' in *Der indische Buddhismus und seine Verzweigungen*. (Die Religionen der Menschheit, vol. 24,1, Verlag W. Kohlhammer, Stuttgart)

Bronkhorst, Johannes (2012), Absorption, Human Nature and Buddhist Liberation. UniversityMedia.

Burkert, Walter (1996), *Creation of the Sacred: Tracks of Biology in Early Religions*. Cambridge, Massuchusetts: Harvard University Press.

Collins, Steven (1982), *Selfless Persons: Imagery and thought in Theravada Buddhism*. Cambridge: Cambridge University Press.

Chamberlain, David (1998), *The Mind of your Newborn Baby*. Berkeley, California: North Atlantic Books.

Dahlbom, Bo (ed.) (1993), *Dennett and his Critics*. Oxford: Blackwell, 1995.

Dennett, Daniel C. (1991), *Consciousness Explained*. Boston: Little, Brown & Co.

Doore, Gary, ed. (1988), Shamans and Healing, Personal Growth and Empowerment, Boston: Shambala.

Dossey, Larry (1997), Be Careful What You Pray For ... you just might get it. San Francisco : Harper.

Dourley, John P. (1996), 'C. G. Jung's appropriation of aspects of shamanism,' in Pentikäinen, 1996.

Downton, J. V. (1989), 'Individuation and Shamanism.' *Journal of Analytical Psychology*, 34, 73-88.

Drury, Nevill (1982), The Shaman and the Magician: Journeys between the worlds. London: Arkana, 1987.

(1989), The Elements of Shamanism. Dorset: Element.

Eliade, Mircea (1958), *Yoga: Immortality and Freedom*. Routledge & Keegan Paul: Bollingen Series LVI. (2nd ed. 1969)

(1960), *Myths, Dreams & Mysteries*. London: Collins, Fontana Library, 1968.

(1964), *Shamanism: Archaic techniques of Ecstasy*. Princeton University Press: Bollingen Series 1972.

Ellenberger, Henri F. (1970), The Discovery of the Unconscious: the History and Evolution of Dynamic Psychology. London: Fontana Press, 1994.

Emerson, V. F. (1972), 'Can Belief Systems Influence Neurophysiology? Some Implications of Research on Meditation.' *Newsletter Review*, the R. M. Bucke Memorial Society, 5:20-32.

Engler, Jack (1984), 'Therapeutic Aims in Psychotherapy and Meditation: Developmental Stages in the Representation of Self.' *Journal of Transpersonal Psychology*, 1984, Vol. 16, No. 1.

Epstein, Mark (1988), 'The Deconstruction of the self: Ego and "Egolessness" in Buddhist Insight Meditation.' *Journal of Transpersonal Psychology*, 1988, Vol. 20, No. 1.

Ergardt, Jan T. (1977) *Faith and Knowledge in Early Buddhism*. Leiden: E. J. Brill.

Frauwallner, E. (1956), *The Earliest Vinaya and the Beginnings of Buddhist Literature*. Serie Orientale Roma, Vol. VIII. Roma: Instituto Italiano per il Medio et Extremo Oriente.

(1956) 'The historical data we possess on the Person and the Doctrine of the Buddha,' in *East and West* 7, pp. 309-312.

Gethin, R.M.L (1986), 'The Five *khandhas*: their treatment in the Nikaayas and early Abhidhamma.' JIP 14 (1986), pp.35-53.

(1992), The Buddhist Path to Awakening: a study of the Bodhi-Pakkhiyaa Dhammaa. Leiden: E. J. Brill.

Gibson, Todd (1997), 'Notes on the History of the Shamanic in Tibet and Inner Asia,' in *Numen*, Vol. 44, pp. 39-59.

Gombrich, Richard (1974), 'Eliade on Buddhism.' *Religious Studies* 10, pp. 225-231.

(1996), How Buddhism Began: the Conditioned Genesis of the Early Teachings. London: Athlone.

Goodman, Felicitas (1990), *Where the Spirits ride the Wind*. Bloomington, IN: Indiana University Press.

Gore, Belinda (1995), Ecstatic Body Postures: an alternate reality workbook. Santa Fe, New Mexico: Bear & Co.

Grof, Stanislav (1988), 'The Shamanic Journey: Observations from Holotropic Therapy,' in Doore, Gary (ed), *Shamans and Healing, Personal Growth and Empowerment*, Boston: Shambala, 1988.

Grof, Stanislav & Christina Grof (eds.) (1989), *Spiritual Emergency: When Personal Transformation Becomes a Crisis*. Los Angeles: Jeremy P. Tarcher.

Grof, Stanislav & Bennett, Hal Zina (1993), The Holotropic Mind: the Three Levels of Human Consciousness and How they shape our Lives. San Francisco: Harper.

Hanegraaff, Wouter J. (1996), New Age Religion and Western Culture: Esotericism in the Mirror of Secular Thought. Leiden: E.J. Brill.

Harner, Michael (1980), *The Way of the Shaman*. San Francisco: Harper and Row.

Hamilton, Sue (1996), Identity and Experience: The Constitution of the Human Being According to Early Buddhism. London: Luzac Oriental, 1996

Hillman, James (1996), The Soul's Code: in Search of Character and Calling. New York: Random House.

Janus, Ludwig (1997), The Enduring Effects of the Prenatal Experience: Echoes from the Womb. Northvale, New Jersey: Jason Aronson, Inc.

Johansson, Rune E. J. (1969) *The Psychology of Nirvana*. London: George Allen and Unwin.

(1979), The Dynamic Psychology of Early Buddhism. Oxford: Curzon Press.

Jung, Carl Gustav (1954) 'The Philosophical Tree,' in *Alchemical Studies*, Collected Works, Vol. 13. Bollingen Series XX. Princeton University Press, 1983.

Kakar, Sudhir (1982), Shamans, Mystics and Doctors: a Psychological Inquiry into India and Its Healing Traditions. London: Unwin Paperbacks.

Kalweit, Holger (1992), *Shamans, Healers, and Medicine Men.* London: Shambala.

Khantiphala, Phra, (2519/1976) *The Splendour of Enlightenment: a Life of theBuddha.* Bankok: Mahaamakut Raajavidyaalaya Press,

Krippner, Stanley & Patrick Welch (1992), Spiritual Dimensions of Healing: from Native Shamanism to Contemporary Health Care. New York: Irvington Publishers, Inc.

Loy, David (1992), 'Avoiding the Void: the *lack* of self in Psychotherapy and Buddhism.' *Journal of Transpersonal Psychology*, 1988, Vol. 24, No. 2.

Manné, Joy (1990), 'Categories of Sutta in the Paali Nikaayas and their implications for our appreciation of the Buddhist Teaching and Literature.= *Journal of the Paali Text Society, XV, 29-87.*

(1992), 'The Digha Nikaya Debates: Debating practices at the time of the Buddha,' Buddhist Studies Review, Vol.9, No.2, 1992.

(1994), 'Rebirthing, an orphan or a member of the family of psychotherapies?' *International Journal of Prenatal and Perinatal Psychology and Medicine,* Vol.6 (1994g), No. 4, 503-517.

(1995), 'Rebirthing, is it marvelous or terrible?' *The Therapist: Journal of the European Therapy Studies Institute*, Spring 1995.

(1995,i), 'Case Histories from the Paali Canon I: the Saamaññaphala Sutta tp case history - or how to be sure to win a debate.' *Journal of the Paali Text Society.*

(1995,ii) 'Case Histories from the Paali Canon II: the Four Stages (*sotaapanna, sakadaagaamin, anaagaamin, arahat*) Case History - spiritual materialism and the need for tangible results.' *Journal of the Paali Text Society.*

(1997) *Soul Therapy.* Berkeley, California: North Atlantic Books.

Ñanamoli, Bhikkhu & Bhikkhu Bodhi (1995), Middle Length Discourses of the Buddha, a new translation of the Majjhima Nikaaya. Boston: Wisdom Publications.

Noel, Daniel C. (1997), The Soul of Shamanism: Western Fantasies, Imaginal Realities. New York: Continuum.

Oetke, Claus (1988), "Ich" und das Ich: Analytische Untersuchungen zur buddhistisch-brahmanischen }tmankontroverse. Stuttgart: Franz Steiner Verlag Wiesbaden GmbH.

Pentikäinen, Juha (ed.), (1996), Shamanism and Northern Ecology. Berlin: Mouton de Gruyter. (Religion and Society 36)

Perry, John Weir (1974), The Far Side of Madness. Dallas: Spring Publications.

Rhys Davids, T.W. & Mrs C.A.F. (1899, 1899, 1921), Dialogues of the Buddha, Vols. I - III. London: Pàli Text Society.

Ripinsky-Naxon, Michael (1993), The Nature of Shamanism: Substance and Function of a Religious Metaphor. Albany: State University of New York Press.

Samuels, Geoffrey (1993), Civilized Shamans: Buddhism in Tibetan Societies. Washington: Smithsonian Institute Press.

Schmithausen Lambert (1997), Maitrii and Magic: Aspects of the Buddhist Attitude Towards the Dangerous in Nature. Wien: Verlag der Österreichishen Akademie der Wissenschaften.

Shamanism, Encyclopedia of Religion, Vol. 13, Editor in Chief, Mircea Eliade. Macmillan: New York, 1987

Siegel, Bernie (1986), Love, Medicine & Miracles. New York: Harper & Row.

Siegel, Lee (1991), Net of Magic: Wonders and Deceptions in India. Chicago: University of Chicago Press.

Staal, Frits (1975), Exploring Mysticism. London: Penguin.

Taylor, Kylea (1994), The Breathwork Experience Exploration and Healing in Nonordinary States of Consciousness. Santa Cruz, CA: Hanford Mead.

Thomas, Edward J. (1927), *The Life of the Buddha as Legend and History*. London: Routledge & Kegan Paul. (3rd ed. 1949)

Vaughan, Frances (1995), Shadows of the Sacred: Seeing through Spiritual Illusions. Wheaton, Illinois: Quest Books.

Wagle, Narendra (1995), *Society at the Time of the Buddha*. Bombay: Popular Prakashan.

Walsh, Roger N. (1989), 'What is a Shaman? Definition, origin and distribution.' *J. Transpersonal Psychology*, Vol. 21, No.1, pp.1-11.

(1990), The Spirit of Shamanism. London: Mandala.

Walshe, Maurice, *The Long Discourses of the Buddha*, a translation of the Diigha Nikaaya. Boston: Wisdom Publications, 1995.

Weil, Andrew (1972), The Natural Mind: a new way of looking at drugs and the higher consciousness. Boston: Houghton Mifflin Company.

Wilbur, Ken (1977), *The Spectrum of Consciousness*. Wheaton, Ill.: Theosophical Publishing House.

(1980) The Atman Project: a transpersonal view of human development. Wheaton, Ill.: Theosophical Publishing House.

(1996), Eye to Eye: the quest for the New Paradigm. Boston: Shambala.

Zafiropulo, Ghiorgo (1993), *L'Ilumination due Buddha: de la Quête à l'Annonce de l'Eveil*. Innsbruck: Verlag des Instituts für Sprachwissenschaft der Universität Innsbruck.

ABBREVIATIONS

APPPAH - Association for Pre- and Perinatal Psychology and Health

DN - Digha Nikaya

ER/S - Shamanism, Encyclopedia of Religion

LDB - Walsh, The Long Discourses of the Buddha

MLDB – Ñañamoli & Bodhi, Middle Length Discourses of the Buddha

MN - Majjhima Nikaya

S - Eliade, *Shamanism*

s. - sutta

Tr./tr. - translation

www.ingramcontent.com/pod-product-compliance
Lightning Source LLC
Chambersburg PA
CBHW070604290526
45790CB00002B/775